THIS BOOK BELONGS TO

<u>Narda Rogers</u>

THE
CLASSIC
TREASURY
of
CHILDREN'S
POETRY

THE
CLASSIC
TREASURY
of
CHILDREN'S
POETRY

EDITED BY LOUISE BETTS EGAN

WITH ILLUSTRATIONS BY RICHARD BERNAL ❧ MARK CORCORAN

DEBBIE DIENEMAN ❧ GARY GIANNI ❧ JOHN GURNEY ❧ BARBARA LANZA

T. LEWIS ❧ MICHAEL MONTGOMERY ❧ ROBYN OFFICER ❧ KAREN PRITCHETT

JIM ROBINSON ❧ JADA ROWLAND

Produced by Ariel Books

COURAGE
BOOKS
An Imprint of

Running Press
Philadelphia, Pennsylvania

Canadian representatives: General Publishing Co., Ltd., 30 Lesmill
Road, Don Mills, Ontario M3B 2T6.

International representatives: Worldwide Media Services, Inc., 115
East Twenty-third Street, New York, New York 10010.

9

Digit on the right indicates the number of this printing.

Library of Congress Cataloging-in-Publication Number
89–83327

ISBN 0–89471–802–9

Printed in Hong Kong
Designed by Susan Hood
Art direction by Michael Hortens

Front cover illustration by Richard Bernal
Front matter illustrations by Karen Pritchett

Illustrations on pages 22 and 23 by Richard Bernal
Illustrations on pages 30, 31, 54 and 55 by Mark Corcoran
Illustrations on pages 48 and 49 by Debbie Dieneman
Illustrations on pages 26, 27, 28, 29, 40 and 41 by Gary Gianni
Illustrations on pages 12, 13, 24, 25, 36 and 37 by John Gurney
Illustrations on pages 50 and 51 by Barbara Lanza
Illustrations on pages 10, 11, 32, 33, 52 and 53 by T. Lewis
Illustrations on pages 14, 15, 20, 21, 38 and 39 by Michael Montgomery
Illustrations on pages 42, 43, 44 and 45 by Robyn Officer
Illustrations on pages 18 and 19 by James Robinson
Illustrations on pages 34, 35, 46 and 47 by Jada Rowland

Published by Courage Books, an imprint of Running Press
Book Publishers, 125 South Twenty-second Street,
Philadelphia, Pennsylvania 19103

Foreword

Poems are like fireworks—they're little packets of verbal energy waiting to be ignited by the human voice. Poems work best when read aloud.

In just a few words or phrases, a good poem can produce colors and excitement, or at least a laugh or smile of recognition. Poems can take an ordinary activity—like listening to the wind, or going to bed—and make it seem magic. Poems can also make fantastic creatures—like fairies or a jabberwocky—spring to life.

Just as a child looks at the world with a certain wonder and curiosity, so does a poem. It presents its subject in an entirely new and fresh perspective, enriching the child's imagination through its colorful phrases and images.

As people grow up, they forget the thrill of rhymes, rhythms, and repeating sounds. Gone are the nonsense poems and characters, and gone is the satisfaction of calling out a verse for the sheer fun of it.

Lucky indeed are the children whose parents keep alive the enchantment first found in nursery rhymes. There is no better way than to read them the poems of the masters.

Louise Betts Egan

CONTENTS

The Rainbow Fairies

Two little clouds, one summer's day,
Went flying through the sky;
They went so fast they bumped their heads,
And both began to cry.

Old Father Sun looked out and said:
"Oh, never mind, my dears,
I'll send my little fairy folk
To dry your falling tears."

One fairy came in violet,
And one wore indigo;
In blue, green, yellow, orange, red,
They made a pretty row.

They wiped the cloud-tears all away,
And then from out the sky,
Upon a line the sunbeams made,
They hung their gowns to dry.

Anonymous

Did You Ever Go Fishing?

Did you ever go fishing on a bright sunny day—
Sit on a fence and have the fence give way?
Slide off the fence and rip your pants,
And see the little fishes do the hootchy-kootchy dance?

Anonymous

Birds of a Feather

Birds of a feather flock together
And so do pigs and swine,
Rats and mice will have their choice,
And so will I have mine.

Anonymous

How Doth . . .

How doth the little crocodile
Improve his shining tail,
And pour the waters of the Nile
On every golden scale!

How cheerfully he seems to grin,
How neatly spreads his claws,
And welcomes little fishes in
With gently smiling jaws!

Lewis Carroll

There Was a Little Girl

There was a little girl, who had a little curl
Right in the middle of her forehead,
And when she was good, she was very, very good,
But when she was bad she was horrid.

Henry Wadsworth Longfellow

13

If You See a Fairy Ring

If you see a fairy ring
In a field of grass,
Very lightly step around,
Tiptoe as you pass;
Last night fairies frolicked there,
And they're sleeping somewhere near.

If you see a tiny fairy
Lying fast asleep,
Shut your eyes and run away,
Do not stay to peep;
And be sure you never tell,
Or you'll break a fairy spell.

Anonymous

The Rainbow

Boats sail on the rivers,
And ships sail on the seas;
But clouds that sail across the sky
Are prettier far than these.

There are bridges on the rivers,
As pretty as you please;
But the bow that bridges heaven,
And overtops the trees,
And builds a road from earth to sky,
Is prettier far than these.

Christina Rossetti

My Dog, Spot

I have a white dog
Whose name is Spot,
And he's sometimes white
And he's sometimes not.
But whether he's white
Or whether he's not,
There's a patch on his ear
That makes him Spot.

He has a tongue
That is long and pink,
And he lolls it out
When he wants to think.
He seems to think most
When the weather is hot.
He's a wise sort of dog,
Is my dog, Spot.

He likes a bone
And he likes a ball,
But he doesn't care
For a cat at all.
He waggles his tail
And he knows what's what,
So I'm glad that he's my dog,
My dog, Spot.

Rodney Bennett

Sam, Sam, the Butcher Man

Sam, Sam, the butcher man,
Washed his face in a frying pan,
Combed his hair with a wagon wheel,
And died with a toothache in his heel.

Anonymous

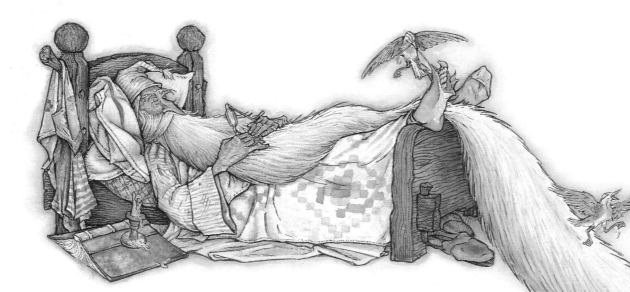

It's Raining, It's Pouring

It's raining, it's pouring,
The old man is snoring;
He went to bed and bumped his head
And couldn't get up in the morning!

Anonymous

There Was an Old Man

There was an Old Man with a beard,
Who said, "It is just as I feared!—
Two Owls and a Hen, four Larks and a Wren,
Have all built their nests in my beard!"

Edward Lear

The Bells

Hear the sledges with the bells—
Silver bells!
What a world of merriment their melody foretells!
How they tinkle, tinkle, tinkle,
In the icy air of night!
While the stars that oversprinkle
All the heavens, seem to twinkle
With a crystalline delight;
Keeping time, time, time,
In a sort of Runic rhyme,
To the tintinnabulation that so musically wells
From the bells, bells, bells, bells,
Bells, bells, bells—
From the jingling and the tinkling of the bells.

Edgar Allan Poe

The Snow

It reaches to the fence,
It wraps it, rail by rail,
Till it is lost in fleeces;
It flings a crystal veil . . .

Emily Dickinson

The Owl and the Pussy-Cat

The Owl and the Pussy-Cat went to sea
In a beautiful pea-green boat,
They took some honey, and plenty of money,
Wrapped up in a five-pound note.
The Owl looked up to the stars above,
And sang to a small guitar,
"O lovely Pussy! O Pussy, my love,
What a beautiful Pussy you are,
      You are,
      You are!
What a beautiful Pussy you are!"

Pussy said to the Owl, "You elegant fowl!
How charmingly sweet you sing!
O let us be married! too long we have tarried:
But what shall we do for a ring?"
They sailed away, for a year and a day,
To the land where the Bong-Tree grows,
And there in a wood a Piggy-wig stood.
With a ring at the end of his nose,
    His nose,
    His nose,
With a ring at the end of his nose.

"Dear Pig, are you willing to sell for one shilling
Your ring?" Said the Piggy, "I will."
So they took it away, and were married next day
By the Turkey who lives on the hill.
They dined on mince, and slices of quince,
Which they ate with a runcible spoon;
And hand in hand, on the edge of the sand,
They danced by the light of the moon,
    The moon,
    The moon,
They danced by the light of the moon.

Edward Lear

The Cats of Kilkenny

There were once two cats of Kilkenny,
Each thought there was one cat too many;
So they fought and they fit,
And they scratched and they bit,
Till, excepting their nails
And the tips of their tails,
Instead of two cats, there weren't any.

Anonymous

The Kitten at Play

See the kitten, how she starts,
Crouches, stretches, paws and darts;
With a tiger-leap half way
Now she meets her coming prey.
Lets it go as fast as then
Has it in her power again.

William Wordsworth

Two Little Kittens

Two little kittens, one stormy night,
Began to quarrel, and then to fight;
One had a mouse, the other had none,
And that's the way the quarrel begun.

Anonymous

Wynken, Blynken, and Nod

Wynken, Blynken, and Nod one night
Sailed off in a wooden shoe—
Sailed on a river of crystal light,
Into a sea of dew.
"Where are you going, and what do you wish?"
The old moon asked the three.
"We have come to fish for the herring fish
That live in this beautiful sea;
Nets of silver and gold have we!"
    Said Wynken,
        Blynken,
           And Nod.

The old moon laughed and sang a song,
As they rocked in the wooden shoe,
And the wind that sped them all night long
Ruffled the waves of dew.
The little stars were the herring fish
That lived in that beautiful sea—
"Now cast your nets wherever you wish—
Never afeard are we";
So cried the stars to the fishermen three:
    Wynken,
       Blynken,
         And Nod.

All night long their nets they threw
To the stars in the twinkling foam—
Then down from the skies came the wooden shoe,
Bringing the fishermen home;

'Twas all so pretty a sail it seemed
As if it could not be,
And some folks thought 'twas a dream they'd dreamed
Of sailing that beautiful sea—
But I shall name you the fishermen three:
    Wynken,
        Blynken,
           And Nod.

Wynken and Blynken are two little eyes,
And Nod is a little head,
And the wooden shoe that sailed the skies
Is a wee one's trundle-bed.
So shut your eyes while mother sings
Of wonderful sights that be,
And you shall see the beautiful things
As you rock in the misty sea,
Where the old shoe rocked the fishermen three:
    Wynken,
        Blynken,
           And Nod.

Eugene Field

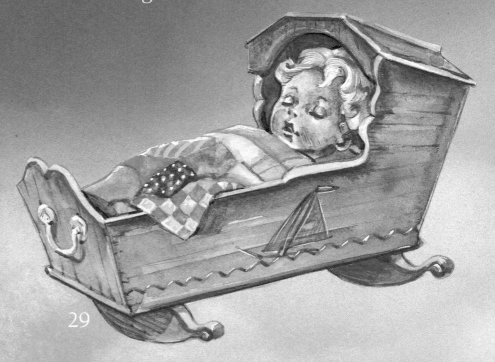

The Snowman

Once there was a snowman
Stood outside the door
Thought he'd like to come inside
And run around the floor;
Thought he'd like to warm himself
By the firelight red;
Thought he'd like to climb up
On that big white bed.
So he called the North Wind, "Help me now I pray.
I'm completely frozen, standing here all day."
So the North Wind came along and blew him in the door,
And now there's nothing left of him
But a puddle on the floor!

Anonymous

Tumbling

In jumping and tumbling
We spend the whole day,
Till night by arriving
Has finished our play.

What then? One and all,
There's no more to be said,
As we tumbled all day,
So we tumble to bed.

Anonymous

Mud

Mud is gooey—
SQUISH patooey!
Mush it with your fingers;
Gush it with your toes.
Slimy, glimy, wet, and grimy—
OooooooooH!
I like mud.

Louise Betts Egan

Kind Deeds

Little drops of water,
Little grains of sand.
Make the mighty ocean,
And the pleasant land.

Thus the little minutes,
Humble though they be,
Make the mighty ages
Of eternity.

Little deeds of kindness,
Little words of love,
Make this earth an Eden
Like the heaven above.

Isaac Watts

Bunny Rabbit

Bunny creeps out and caresses his nose,
Combs out his ears with his fluttering toes,
Blinks at the sun
And commences to run
With a skip and a hop
And a flippety-flop,
Nibbling the clover wherever he goes;
But only when he is quite easy in mind
Does he button his little white tail down behind.

Anonymous

The Little Moon

The night is come, but not too soon,
And sinking silently,
All silently, the little moon
Drops down behind the sky.

Henry Wadsworth Longfellow

Star Light, Star Bright . . .

Star light, star bright,
First star I've seen tonight,
Wish I may, wish I might,
Have this wish I wish tonight.

Anonymous

Algy Met a Bear

Algy met a bear,
A bear met Algy.
The bear was bulgy,
The bulge was Algy.

Anonymous

Way Down South

Way down South where bananas grow,
A grasshopper stepped on an elephant's toe.
The elephant said, with tears in his eyes,
"Pick on somebody your own size."

Anonymous

A Fly and a Flea in a Flue

A fly and a flea in a flue
Were imprisoned, so what could they do?
Said the fly, "Let us flee!"
"Let us fly!" said the flea,
And they flew through a flaw in the flue.

Anonymous

I Asked My Mother

I asked my mother for fifty cents
To see the elephant jump the fence.
He jumped so high that he touched the sky
And never came back till the Fourth of July.

Anonymous

Foreign Lands

Up into the cherry-tree
Who should climb but little me?
I held the trunk with both my hands
And looked abroad on foreign lands.

I saw the next-door garden lie,
Adorned with flowers before my eye,
And many pleasant places more
That I had never seen before.

I saw the dimpling river pass
And be the sky's blue looking-glass;
The dusty roads go up and down
With people tramping in to town.

If I could find a higher tree
Farther and farther I should see,
To where the grown-up river slips
Into the sea among the ships,

To where the roads on either hand
Lead onward into fairy land,
Where all the children dine at five,
And all the playthings come alive.

Robert Louis Stevenson

The Wind

Who has seen the wind?
Neither I nor you;
But when the leaves hang trembling
The wind is passing through.

Who has seen the wind?
Neither you nor I;
But when the trees bow down their heads
The wind is passing by.

Christina Rossetti

Spring Is Showery

Spring is showery, flowery, bowery;
Summer is hoppy, croppy, poppy;
Autumn is wheezy, sneezy, freezy;
Winter is slippy, drippy, nippy.

Anonymous

The March Wind

I come to work as well as play;
I'll tell you what I do;
I whistle all the live-long day,
"Woo-oo-oo-oo! Woo-oo!"

I toss the branches up and down
And shake them to and fro,
I whirl the leaves in flocks of brown,
And send them high and low.

I strew the twigs upon the ground,
The frozen earth I sweep;
I blow the children round and round
And wake the flowers from sleep.

Anonymous

The Fly-Away Horse

Oh, a wonderful horse is the Fly-Away Horse—
Perhaps you have seen him before;
Perhaps, while you slept, his shadow has swept
Through the moonlight that floats on the floor.
For it's only at night, when the stars twinkle bright,
That the Fly-Away Horse, with a neigh
And a pull at his rein and a toss of his mane,
Is up on his heels and away!
The Moon in the sky,
As he gallops by,
Cries: "Oh! what a marvellous sight!"
And the Stars in dismay
Hide their faces away
In the lap of old Grandmother Night.

It is yonder, out yonder, the Fly-Away Horse
Speedeth ever and ever away—
Over meadows and lanes, over mountains and plains,
Over streamlets that sing at their play;
And over the sea like a ghost sweepeth he,
While the ships they go sailing below,
And he speeds so fast that the men at the mast
Adjudge him some portent of woe.

"What ho, there!" they cry,
As he flourishes by
With a whisk of his beautiful tail;
And the fish in the sea
Are as scared as can be,
From the nautilus up to the whale!

And the Fly-Away Horse seeks those far-away lands
You little folk dream of at night—
Where candy-trees grow, and honey-brooks flow,
And cornfields with popcorn are white;
And the beasts in the wood are ever so good
To children who visit them there—
What glory astride of a lion to ride,
Or to wrestle around with a bear!
The monkeys, they say:
"Come on, let us play,"
And they frisk in the coconut trees:
While the parrots that cling
To the peanut vines sing
Or converse with comparative ease!

Off! scamper to bed—you shall ride him tonight!
For, as soon as you've fallen asleep,
With jubilant neigh he shall bear you away
Over forest and hillside and deep!
But tell us, my dear, all you see and you hear
In those beautiful lands over there,
Where the Fly-Away Horse wings his far-away course
With the wee one consigned to his care.
Then Grandma will cry
In amazement: "Oh, my!"
And she'll think it could never be so.
And only we two
Shall know it is true—
You and I, little precious! shall know!

Eugene Field

45

A Calendar

January brings the snow,
Makes our feet and fingers glow.

February brings the rain,
Thaws the frozen lake again.

March brings breezes, loud and shrill,
To stir the dancing daffodil.

April brings the primrose sweet,
Scatters daisies at our feet.

May brings flocks of pretty lambs,
Skipping by their fleecy dams.

June brings tulips, lilies, roses,
Fills the children's hands with posies.

Weather

Whether the weather be fine
Or whether the weather be not,
Whether the weather be cold
Or whether the weather be hot,
We'll weather the weather
Whatever the weather,
Whether we like it or not.

Anonymous

Hot July brings cooling showers,
Apricots and gillyflowers.

August brings the sheaves of corn,
Then the harvest home is borne.

Warm September brings the fruit;
Sportsmen then begin to shoot.

Fresh October brings the pheasant;
Then to gather nuts is pleasant.

Dull November brings the blast;
Then the leaves are whirling fast.

Chill December brings the sleet,
Blazing fire, and Christmas treat.

Sara Coleridge

Thirty Days Hath September

Thirty days hath September,
April, June, and November;
All the rest have thirty-one,
Excepting February alone,
And that has twenty-eight days clear
And twenty-nine in each leap year.

Anonymous

The Swing

How do you like to go up in a swing,
Up in the air so blue?
Oh, I do think it the pleasantest thing
Ever a child can do!

Up in the air and over the wall
Till I can see so wide,
Rivers and trees and cattle and all
Over the countryside—

Till I look down on the garden green,
Down on the roof so brown—
Up in the air I go flying again,
Up in the air and down!

Robert Louis Stevenson

If I Could Fly

I wish I had wings,
So I could fly,
Wherever, whenever,
However high.

Over the schoolyard,
Over the pond,
I'd fly to the clouds,
And way beyond!

Birds might well wonder
Who I could be,
Kicking and spinning,
And shouting out, "Wheee!"

I'd float on the air
And wave to the ground;
I'd jump off a swing,
And zoom up, uP, UP—
          Not
                    down.

I'd soar with the wind
As far as it goes,
And tickle the treetops
With my bare toes.

Louise Betts Egan

There Was an Old Woman

There was an old woman tossed up in a basket
Nineteen times as high as the moon;
Where she was going I couldn't but ask it,
For in her hand she carried a broom.

"Old woman, old woman, old woman," said I,
"Oh where, Oh where, Oh where, so high?"
"To brush the cobwebs off the sky!"
"Shall I go with you?" "Yes, by-and by."

Anonymous

The Robin

When up aloft
I fly and fly,
I see in pools
The shining sky,
And a happy bird
Am I, am I!

Thomas Hardy

Bug in a Jug

Curious fly,
Vinegar jug,
Slippery edge,
Pickled bug.

Anonymous

Hurt No Living Thing

Hurt no living thing;
Ladybird, nor butterfly,
Nor moth with dusty wing,
Nor cricket chirping cheerily,
Nor grasshopper so light of leap,
Nor dancing gnat, nor beetle fat,
Nor harmless worms that creep.

Christina Rossetti

The Owl

There was an old owl who lived in an oak;
The more he heard, the less he spoke.
The less he spoke, the more he heard.
Why aren't we like that wise old bird?

Anonymous

Bedtime

The evening is coming,
The sun sinks to rest;
The rooks are all flying
Straight home to the nest.
"Caw!" says the rook, as he flies overhead;
"It's time little people were going to bed!"

Good-night, little people,
Good-night, and good-night;
Sweet dreams to your eyelids
Till dawning of light;
The evening has come, there's no more to be said;
It's time little people were going to bed!

Thomas Hood

Now the Day Is Over

Now the day is over,
Night is drawing nigh,
Shadows of the evening
Steal across the sky.

Now the darkness gathers,
Stars begin to peep,
Birds and beasts and flowers
Soon will be asleep.

Sabine Baring-Gould

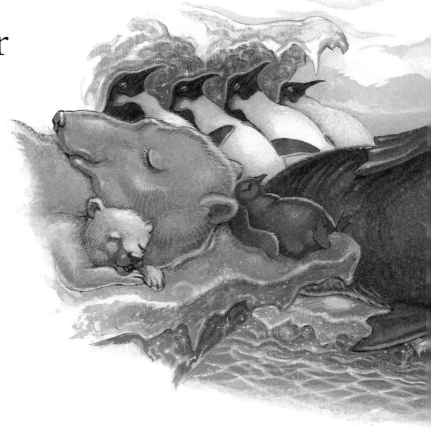

Bed in Summer

In winter I get up at night
And dress by yellow candle-light.
In summer, quite the other way,
I have to go to bed by day.

I have to go to bed and see
The birds still hopping on the tree,
Or hear the grown-up people's feet
Still going past me in the street.

And does it not seem hard to you,
When all the sky is clear and blue,
And I should like so much to play,
To have to go to bed by day?

Robert Louis Stevenson

A Child's Thought

At seven, when I go to bed,
I find such pictures in my head:
Castles with dragons prowling round,
Gardens where magic fruits are found;
Fair ladies prisoned in a tower,
Or lost in an enchanted bower;
While gallant horsemen ride by streams
That border all this land of dreams
I find, so clearly in my head
At seven, when I go to bed.

Robert Louis Stevenson